Thanksgiving

Thanksgiving was first observed by the Pilgrims in the year 1621. The Pilgrims had just survived their first difficult winter in the new settlement near present-day Provincetown, Massachusetts. The Pilgrims made friends with the Native Americans who taught them to build stronger houses and hunt for food. When spring arrived, the Pilgrims went to work plowing the land and planting seeds brought from England. One Native American, Squanto, became especially helpful to the Pilgrims.

When harvest time came, the Pilgrims discovered that they had more than enough produce to store for the next winter. The Pilgrims were so grateful that they decided to hold a feast of thanksgiving, inviting their Native American friends. The Native Americans brought shellfish, game, and wild turkeys. The Pilgrims filled the tables with bounty from their gardens. They all bowed their heads and said a prayer of thanks to God before beginning the feast which lasted three days.

Today, Thanksgiving is celebrated in America on the fourth Thursday of November. Families gather together to share a special meal and to thank God for all the good that has been given them.

Activities

Grouping Turkey Feathers: Buy a package of brightly colored feathers (found in craft stores). Have children group the feathers that are alike in color.

Building Log Cabins: Build some log cabins for the Pilgrim family out of wooden building logs. Make a Pilgrim family. Stand up the characters to complete the scene!

Making Foam and Pipe-Cleaner Turkeys: Spray paint a foam ball brown. Let dry. Push in colored pipe cleaners for turkey feathers and feet. (Remember to spray paint outside or in a well-ventilated area.)

Stringing Popcorn Necklaces: Provide each child with a needle and strong cotton thread approximately 20 " (50 cm) long, and popcorn flakes. Tie off the two ends of the thread when the necklace is long enough to go over the child's head.

Comparing Thanksgivings: Read a book that tells about the first Thanksgiving and the conditions under which the Pilgrims lived. Make a Venn diagram or a chart comparing Thanksgiving then and now.

Bibliography

Accorsi, William. *Friendship's First Thanksgiving*. Holiday LB, 1992.

Balian, Lorna. *Sometimes It's Turkey—Sometimes It's Feathers*. Humbug Books, 1987.

Brown, Marc. *Arthur's Thanksgiving*. Little, 1983.

Bunting, Eve. *A Turkey for Thanksgiving*. Houghton, 1991.

Dalgliesh, Alice. *The Thanksgiving Story*. Macmillan, 1988.

Dragonwater, Crescent. *Alligator Arrived with Apples: A Potluck Alphabet Feast*. Macmillan, 1987.

Miller, Mary Beth and George Ancona. *Handtalk School*. Macmillan, 1991.

Prelutsky, Jack. *It's Thanksgiving*. Scholastic, 1989.

Oh, What a Thanksgiving!

Author: Steven Kroll

Publisher: Scholastic, 1988 *(available in Canada from Scholastic; in UK, Scholastic Limited; in AUS, Ashton Scholastic Party Limited)*

Summary: A young boy named David uses his imagination to find out what it would have been like if he could have been at the first Thanksgiving feast.

Related Holiday: Thanksgiving has been celebrated as a national holiday in the United States since 1863. It is held on the last Thursday in November as a reminder of the first Thanksgiving celebrated in 1621.

Related Poetry: "Thanksgiving" by Myra Cohn Livingston, *Celebrations* (Scholastic, 1985)

Related Songs: "Hurray, It's Thanksgiving Day!" by Jean Warren and "Thanksgiving Day Thanks" by Patricia Coyne, *Holiday Piggyback Songs* (Warren Publishing House, Inc., 1988)

Connecting Activities

❑

Before reading the story, discuss with children facts that they know about the first Thanksgiving. Compare our present-day Thanksgiving with the first Thanksgiving celebration. How has Thanksgiving changed? How has it remained the same?

❑

After reading the story, make some comparison charts to review certain elements found in the plot. To make the posters, draw a line down the center of three 12" x 18" (30 cm x 45 cm) pieces of white construction paper or tagboard. Compare the *Mayflower* and the bus, the cottage and David's house, and the hunting trip and the shopping trip. Make a list of similarities and differences.

❑

Food is an important part of every Thanksgiving celebration. Ask the children what types of foods they enjoy on Thanksgiving Day. Then find out what the Pilgrims and Native Americans had to eat. Some good factual references are *The Pilgrims' First Thanksgiving* by Ann McGovern, *Sarah Morton's Day: A Day in the Life of a Pilgrim Girl* by Kate Waters and *Samuel Eaton's Day: A Day in the Life of a Pilgrim Boy* also by Kate Waters. Fold some 9" x 12" (23 cm x 30 cm) pieces of light-colored construction paper in half to make menus. List and illustrate a menu for the first Thanksgiving. Do the same for a modern day menu. Encourage the children to add lots of details in their descriptions of the foods and the pictures. Show some real restaurant menus to help in designing the Thanksgiving menus. For example, one entree for the Pilgrims' menu might read: Classic Cornbread—delicious homemade bread baked the old-fashioned way.

Oh, What a Thanksgiving! *(cont.)*

❑

Cut out large letters approximately 15" (38 cm) tall out of tagboard or construction paper. Spell the word *Thanksgiving* or *November.* Divide the children into partners or small groups and distribute the letters. For each letter, the children need to think of a theme that relates to the Thanksgiving season. The letters are then decorated with cutout pictures made from construction paper. For example, the letters might be decorated with paper turkeys, Pilgrims, feathers, or colorful fall leaves.

❑

For a colorful decoration that also enhances self-esteem, first put up a large paper turkey on the wall, without the tail feathers. Explain to the children that in November you are launching a special project called "Feathers for Fred." Fred the turkey has lost all his tail feathers and needs to grow some more before Thanksgiving. The children can help Fred regain feathers for his tail by following rules, completing work, being a good friend, or whatever criteria are set. In order for each child to feel a part of the activity, give each child the same number of feathers. It is then the adult's job to "catch" each child being good and to give a boost of self-esteem while awarding the feathers. A positive comment can be written on the feathers which can be taken down at the end of the month and made into a Native American headband.

❑

To emphasize a spirit of cooperation and good behavior, fill out a "Thankful Certificate" for each child. The adult completes the award by filling in the page with a comment such as "I am thankful that you were a good friend" or "I am thankful that your work showed improvement." The certificates are awarded at the end of the month and can be presented as part of a celebration feast.

❑

Make Pilgrim hats and Native American headbands and have the children pretend that they are at the first Thanksgiving feast. Work with your children to cook some traditional foods, such as pumpkin pie, cornbread, homemade butter, and cranberry sauce (even a turkey with stuffing!). Or serve some healthy snacks (popcorn, raisins, etc.) as part of your feast. Do a picture graph to find out what the favorite food was at the feast.

❑

The first Thanksgiving was characterized by a spirit of sharing and cooperation. Encourage those feelings by helping others during the Thanksgiving season. You might donate some of the foods you bake to an agency that helps the homeless in your community. Or, hold a bake sale and use the money collected to buy a turkey to give to a needy family. Many agencies have lists of people who are "adopted" for the holidays and are provided with all the food necessary for a Thanksgiving dinner. Organize a canned food drive in your school and collect donations in paper bags during the first two weeks of November

Thanksgiving Coupon Book

Carefully color, cut out, and staple the coupons into book form. On Thanksgiving Day, give them to someone you are thankful for.

Happy Thanksgiving from

_____

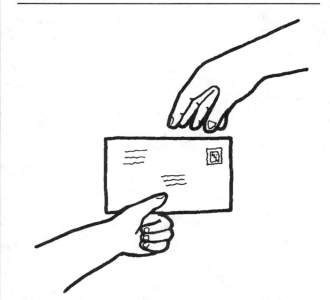

This is good for one errand.

Happy Thanksgiving from

_____

This is good for one hug.

Happy Thanksgiving from

_____

This is good for feeding a pet.

Happy Thanksgiving from

_____

This is good for helping with the dishes.

Happy Thanksgiving from

_____

This is good for setting the table.

Happy Thanksgiving from

_____

This is good for taking out the trash.

Happy Thanksgiving from

_____

This is good for helping with dinner.

Happy Thanksgiving from

_____

This is good for being cheerful all day.

Colorful Turkey

Name_____

Color by numbers.

1 (orange)   3 (red)   5 (brown)
2 (blue)   4 (yellow)   6 (green)

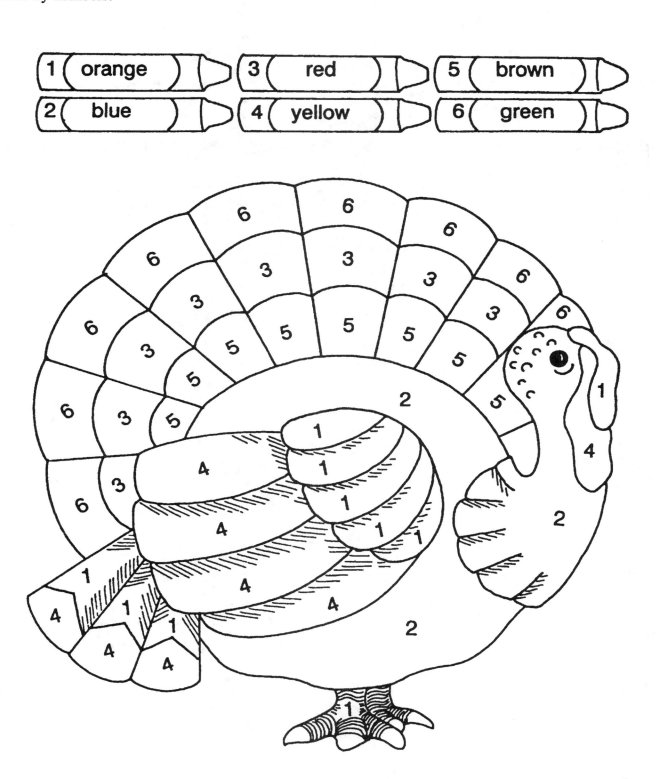

A-Maizing Art

Materials:

- scissors
- tagboard
- glue
- colored popcorn or 1/4" (.6 cm) squares of yellow, orange, and brown construction paper
- maize shape
- husk shape
- brown crepe paper or construction paper

Directions:

Cut out the maize shape and glue to tagboard. Glue colored popcorn or construction paper squares to the shape. Make two or three husks from brown construction paper. Attach these husks to the back of the maize.

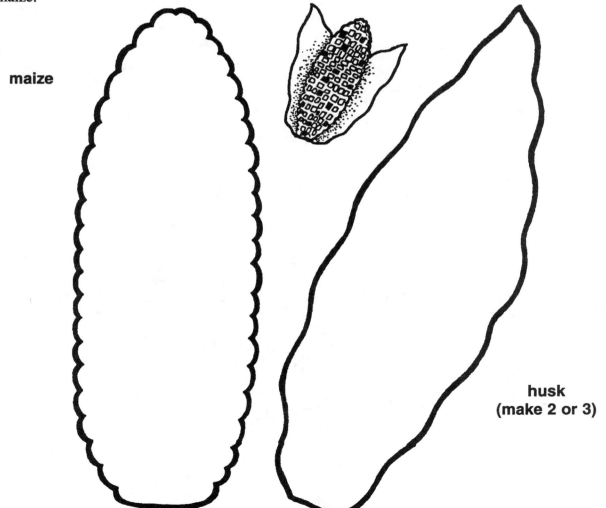

maize

husk
(make 2 or 3)

Thanksgiving Candle Holder

Materials:

- small baby-food jar
- enamel spray paint
- large wooden ring or bead
- small candle
- markers or crayons
- glue
- scissors
- plaster of Paris
- glitter (optional)

Directions:

1. Pour plaster of Paris into a baby-food jar and insert the candle into the center of the jar.
2. Spray the jar and plaster of Paris top with color of your choice.
3. Slide a bead down over the candle to the plaster top.
4. Reproduce, color, and cut out one of the following candle-holder designs. Glue the design around the baby-food jar.
5. Optional: Add glitter to the candle holder.

Shape Turkey

Materials:

- the shapes below
- orange and brown construction paper
- scrap of red construction paper

Directions:

1. Cut out the different shapes below.
2. From the brown paper make two rectangles for feathers and one large brown circle for the body.
3. From the orange paper make the head, the beak, two feet, and two rectangles for feathers.
4. Use the red to cut the oval for the wattle.
5 Have children assemble the turkey, drawing in the details.

Tessy Turkey Earring/Ring Box

Materials:

- small gelatin or pudding box
- markers or crayons
- scissors
- glue
- enamel spray paint

Directions:

1. Cut the box on top of the long side to make an opening. This is where the rings and earrings are stored. Spray the box brown.

2. Reproduce, color, and cut out the turkey pieces.

3. Fold turkey head in half. Fold tabs upwards. Glue turkey heads together, back to back. Apply glue under tabs and glue the turkey head to one end of the box. (See picture diagram.)

4. Apply glue to the tabs at the bottoms of the turkey feathers. Glue these feathers to the back end of the box. (See picture diagram.)

5. Glue one wing to each side of the box.

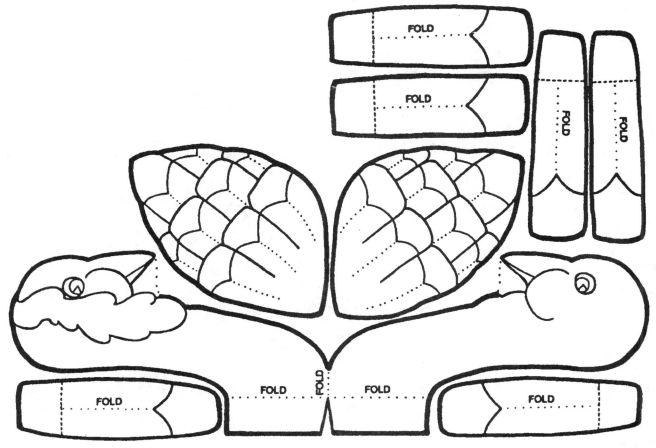

Oh, What a Feast!

On the Thanksgiving dinner plate, draw and color all your favorite Thanksgiving Day foods.

Thanksgiving Napkin Rings

Materials:

- markers or crayons
- scissors
- glue
- toilet paper tube

Directions:

1. Cut a toilet paper tube into four equal parts.

2. Reproduce napkin ring patterns below onto white construction paper. Color and cut out the napkin ring patterns.

3. Apply glue to the wrong side of each pattern and form a ring shape around each toilet tube piece. (See diagram.)

4. Put paper or cloth napkins in the rings for a Thanksgiving gift!

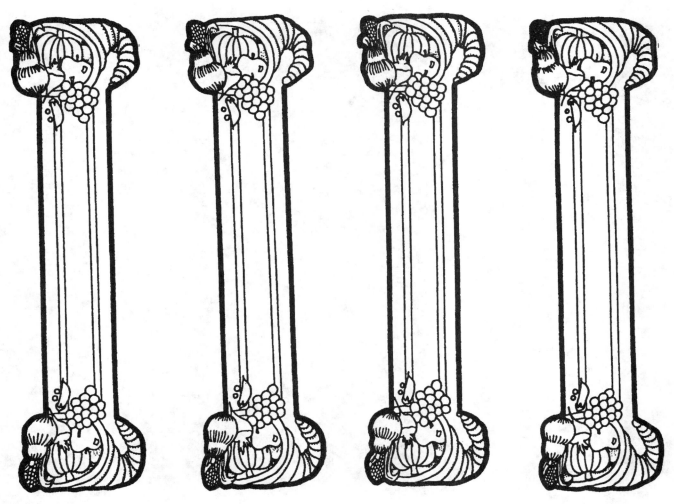

Matching Feathers

Directions:

1. Cut out and paste the dotted feathers on the following page to the matching numbers on the turkey.

2. Color the turkey.

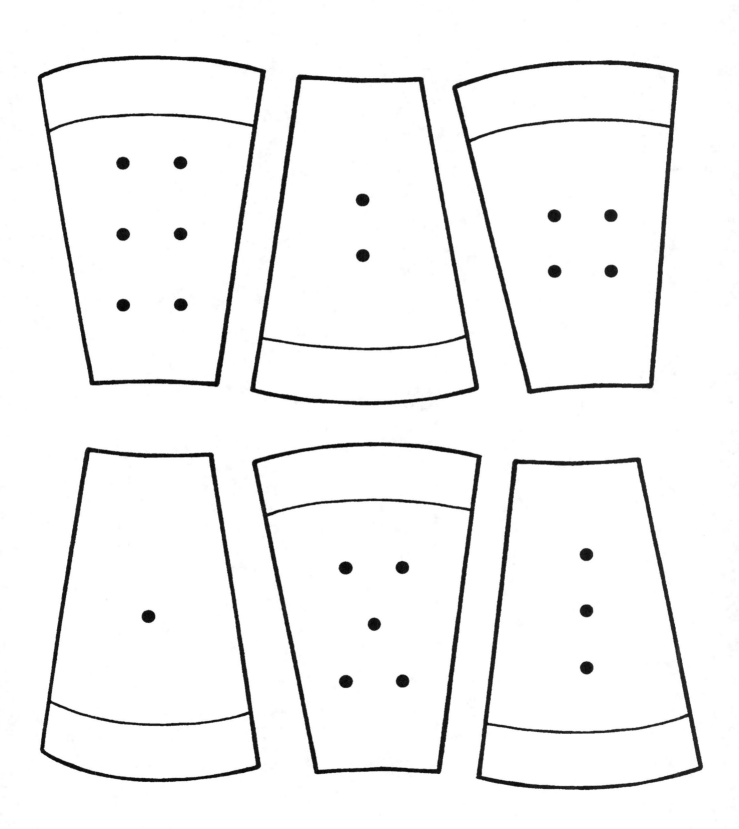

The First Thanksgiving

During the first Thanksgiving feast, popcorn was given to the Pilgrims as a gift by a Native American named Quadequina. Can you find the 15 hidden popcorn flakes? As you find them, color them in.

Thankful Certificates

THANKFUL CERTIFICATE

I am thankful that _____

Child's Name

_____

_____

_____   _____
Date   *Teacher's Signature*

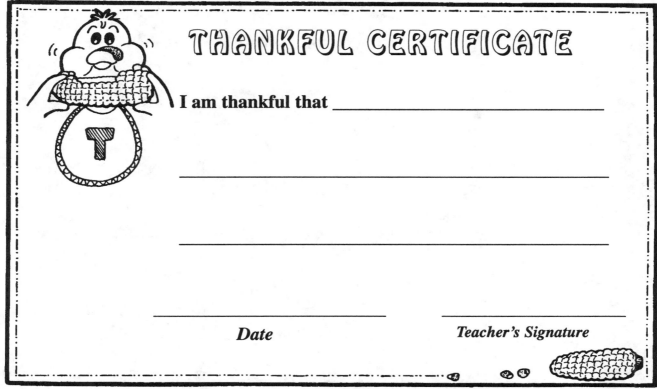

THANKFUL CERTIFICATE

I am thankful that _____

_____

_____

_____   _____
Date   *Teacher's Signature*